CONTRIBUTORS

John E. Allen

Sue Becklake

Robert Burton

Barry Cox

Jacqueline Dineen

Plantagenet Somerset Fry

Bill Gunston

Robin Kerrod

Kaye Orten

Peter Stephens

Aubrey Tulley

Tom Williamson

Thomas Wright

ARTISTS

Jim Bamber / Roger Phillips

John Bilham / Peter Robinson

Jeffrey Burns / Chris Simmons

Dick Eastland / Andrew Skilleter

John Frazer / Raymond Turvey

Elizabeth Graham-Yool

Colin Hawkins

Richard Hook

Illustra

Eric Jewell

Ben Manchipp

Peter North

Photo Credits
British Museum; Werner Forman Archive; French Government Tourist Office; Michael Holford; Picturepoint Ltd; Staatliche Museum de Berlin.
Front Cover: Michael Holford

CHIEF EDUCATIONAL ADVISER

Lynda Snowdon
Infant School Headteacher

TEACHER ADVISORY PANEL

Helen Craddock
Infant School Headteacher

John Enticknap
Author and Primary School Headteacher

Arthur Razzell
Lecturer in Child Development, Author and Headteacher

EDITORIAL BOARD

Philip M. Clark   Executive Editor
Rosemary Canter   Editor
Ethel Hurwicz   Picture Researcher

DESIGNERS

Faulkner/Marks

© Macmillan Publishers Limited, 1979

First Published in 1979 by
Macmillan Children's Books
a division of Macmillan Publishers Limited,
4 Little Essex Street, London WC2R 3LF
and Basingstoke

ISBN 0 333 252764 (Volume 6)
     0 333 194446 (Complete Set)

Printed in Hong Kong

People of Long Ago

Contents

THE FIRST MEN AND WOMEN

These people lived thirty thousand years ago. Their skeletons were found at Cromagnon in France, so they are called Cromagnon people. From their skeletons, we know what they looked like. The people who lived before the Cromagons were much shorter and had smaller brains.

The Cromagnons hunted deer for food and made clothes from animal skins. The man on the left is making sewing needles from animal horns.

The discovery of fire

People have used fire for thousands of years. We do not know how they learned to use it. Perhaps they discovered it by chance when two stones were struck together and made a spark. The spark may have set light to grass near by. Perhaps people worked out other ways to make fire, like the ways shown below.

People had seen fires long before they discovered how to make fire themselves. They saw trees set on fire by lightning.

One way to make fire is to roll a pointed stick in a flat piece of wood.

Another way to make fire is to rub a stick up and down a groove in a piece of wood. After a long time the stick begins to smoulder and smoke.

Fires burning in caves made the caves warm and kept them dry. People burned big fires at night to stop wild animals coming in.

2

In very dry warm weather woodlands sometimes caught fire. When this happened, people became frightened, and ran away.

3

Once men learned to make fire, they could cook their food. They cooked meat on beds of pine needles and made ovens from pebbles and clay.

5

Wild animals were afraid of fire. These men are driving away a fierce animal by using long burning sticks to frighten it.

6

When people began farming, they used fire to clear spaces to plant crops. The wood ashes made the land give extra good crops.

The first homes

The earliest people lived in the hot parts of the world, like Africa. They sheltered in caves in mountains or hills. The caves they chose were near rivers, lakes or springs. Later people made huts of mud, grass or reeds.

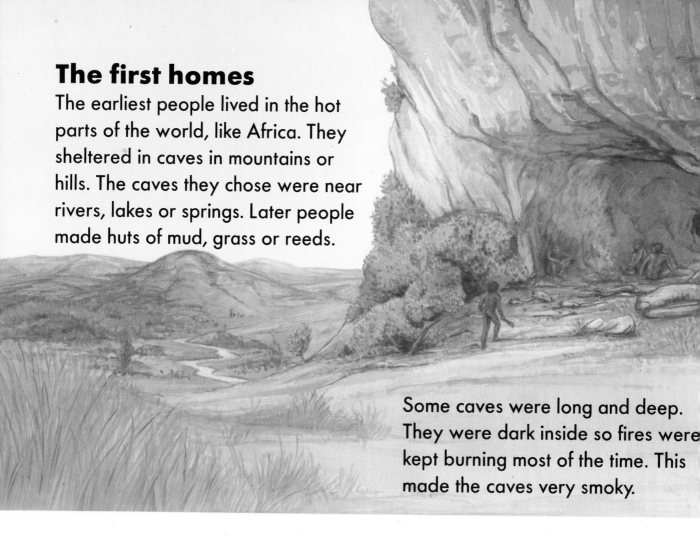

Some caves were long and deep. They were dark inside so fires were kept burning most of the time. This made the caves very smoky.

Then people learned how to make round houses from blocks of earth o animal skins. The animal bones at the bottom made the huts stronger.

As time went by, people made better huts. These people have put animal skins around simple wooden frames. These huts were like tents.

Some people still build huts with wooden frames. This picture shows a hut in a jungle clearing in modern Papua New Guinea.

Gathering food

This is a village in Europe, about three thousand years ago. The people were very good farmers. They grew corn and vegetables, and kept pigs, cattle and sheep. They built canoes and went fishing on the lake.

CRAFTS AND TOOLS

The first tools people used were probably sticks, stones and bones which they picked up from the ground. Then they found they could use one flint or stone to chip another and make a sharp cutting edge. Later they improved these stone tools by tying them to wooden handles. Some tools were made of bone.

These people are using tools for different purposes. A woman is cutting up animal skins to make clothes. Another woman is punching holes in a piece of skin. Behind them, a man and boy are making animal skins into a tent.

People used flintstone to make their stone tools. They dug deep pits in the ground and chipped out chunks of hard flint. Then they broke it into flakes that had sharp edges. These tools had many uses.

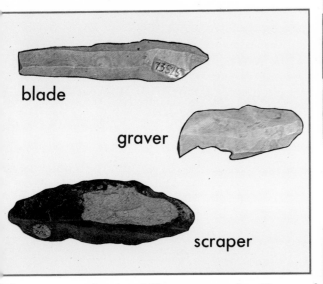

blade

graver

scraper

These are three different tools. One of them was for carving. The scraper was used for cleaning leather. The graver was used to make holes in leather.

The first metal that people used was copper. Here is a copper axe head. Later, they made a harder metal called bronze. Bronze is a mixture of copper and tin.

Men made the first tools using wood, deer antlers and stone.

First they shaped the flint roughly by striking it with a piece of antler.

Then they carefully flaked away the sides of the flint to sharpen the tip.

This flint blade was used as a spear head or as a dagger.

The first pottery

People made pots for cooking and for storing food more than eight thousand years ago. They made the pots from clay, which was dug out of the ground. To make them hard, the pots were baked in a fire. Later, people decorated their pots. At first they just made patterns. Then they painted pictures on the pots.

This woman is showing her son how to dig up clay with a wooden tool. She uses her hands to squeeze the lumps of clay into balls.

The woman rolls each ball of clay between her hands to form a clay stick. If the clay is dry or stiff, she mixes it with water. This makes the clay easier to work.

To form the pot, the woman coils the stick round and round and up into a spiral shape. One clay stick makes a small pot. Larger pots need two or more sticks of clay.

Next the woman smoothes the outside and the inside of the pot, pressing the clay gently into shape.

Now the pot must be baked hard in a fire. When the clay starts to go darker, the pot is left to cool.

This pot was found in Egypt. A pattern of birds was painted on it before it was baked hard.

This pot is decorated with a pattern of grooves. The grooves were made by a pointed stick on the soft clay.

The first clothes

The first people were hunters. They dressed in animal skins, like this Cromagnon man. He is wearing a leather shirt, skirt and boots. In later times, people became farmers. They kept sheep for their meat and wool. The wool was used for clothes. It was warmer than leather animal skins.

The pictures below show how early people made clothes. They used the skins of large animals, like this bison.

First the skin was cleaned. Then it was pegged out on the ground and left to dry.

The skin was then cut out. Holes were made along the edges. The pieces were sewn together with dried grass or leather strips.

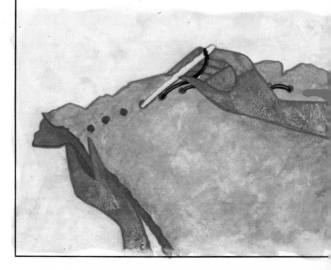

The Ancient Egyptians grew flax and cotton and made cloth from them. They wove the yarn on a loom.

loom

This Egyptian woman is holding a mirror of polished bronze. She is outlining her eyes with black kohl.

Both men and women wore jewellery in Ancient Egypt. Some of the jewellery, like the pendant, was worn for good luck.

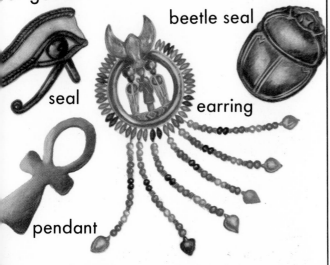

beetle seal

seal

earring

pendant

This woman lived in Egypt more than three thousand years ago. Because it was very hot in Egypt she is wearing light, loose clothes made of linen. Her feet are bare. Rich women like her often wore gold or silver jewellery. Besides wearing bracelets, earrings and a necklace, her hair is decorated with beads.

The first painting

The Cromagnons were the first people we know about who painted pictures. They painted pictures of the animals they hunted on cave walls. They thought the paintings would bring them luck in the hunt. On the right is part of a painting found on the wall of a cave in France.

Cavemen made paint with powder from coloured rock, mixed with water or animal fat. Their paintbrushes were sticks and brushes of animal hair.

Sometimes cavemen painted this way. First they soaked the cave wall with water. Then they blew coloured powder at the wall through a tube.

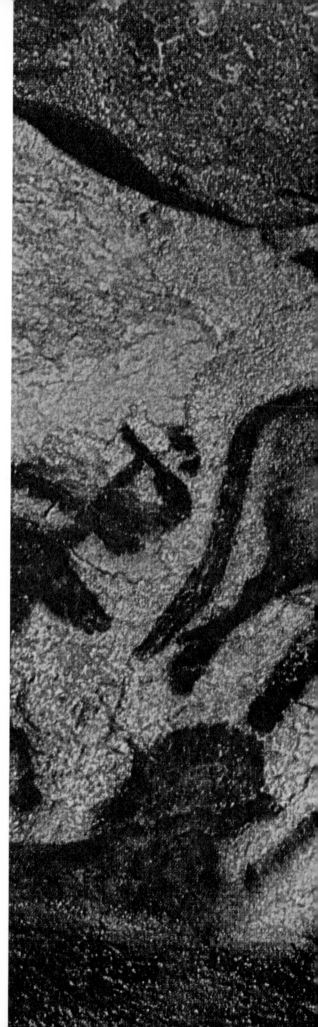

The first writing

We have learned a lot about people of long ago from their writings. The first people to write things down were the Sumerians. They used picture signs. People in different parts of the world invented their own picture signs. You can see some Egyptian writing, called hieroglyphics, in the picture on the right.

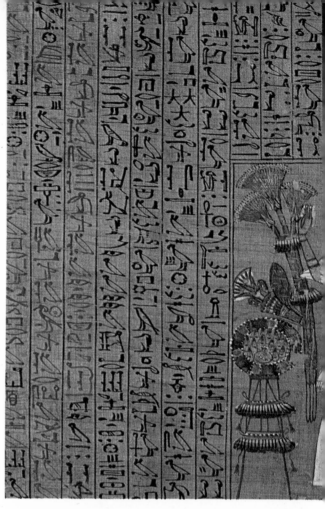

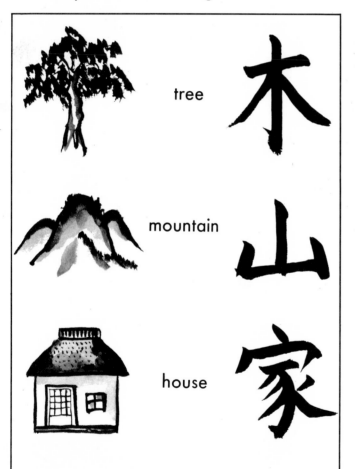

tree

mountain

house

木 山 家

Chinese writing was also in picture signs. Here are some modern Chinese picture signs and the things they stand for.

At first, the Chinese scratched or painted their writing on bones or wood. Then they invented a kind of paper made from rags.

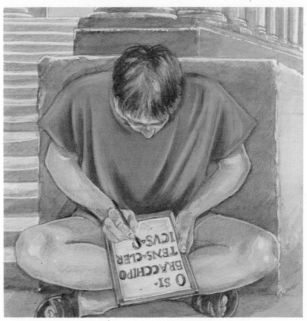

The Sumerians used wedge shapes to form their writing signs. They cut out the shapes on a special tool, which they pressed on to clay tablets.

In Roman times, people wrote by scratching on wax-covered tablets. They used a pointed metal tool called a stylus.

EARLY CIVILIZATIONS

The Sumerians

The Sumerians lived in Mesopotamia over five thousand years ago. They farmed the rich land between the River Tigris and the River Euphrates. Some Sumerians lived in cities. One city, called Ur, has been excavated. Many treasures were found.

The Sumerians wore colourful clothes. You can see their clothes in the picture on the left.

The Sumerians built huge temples, called ziggurats. This one was built at Ur. At the very top of the staircase there was a place to worship.

This model of a goat caught in a bush was found at Ur. It is made of gold and precious stones.

Sumerian buildings were made of clay bricks. First, men trampled on lumps of clay to mix them together.

The clay was shaped into long thin bricks. These were left in the hot sun until they were baked hard.

Then the bricks were built up in rows. Sumerian brick buildings lasted a very long time.

A sphinx was a legendary monster. The Egyptians thought the monster was a lion with a man's head. This is a statue of a sphinx.

The Egyptians

Every year, the River Nile in Egypt flooded. This made the land around the river very fertile. The Egyptians began to farm this land over six thousand years ago. They grew fruit, barley, vegetables, wheat and vines.

The Egyptians made special coffins for their kings and queens. The coffins were shaped like the human body. This one is richly decorated.

The Egyptians buried their dead kings, called pharaohs, in pyramid. All the pharaoh's treasures were buried with him. Thousands of slav were needed to build the pyramid

The slaves used ropes to drag the huge blocks of stone up the pyramids. In this picture the architect is displaying his plans.

The Minoans

The Minoans of Crete were named after a legendary king called King Minos. Four and a half thousand years ago, the Minoans were farmers and traders. They traded by sea with other people in the Mediterranean, carrying goods in huge pottery jars.

One ancient Greek legend said that King Minos kept a fierce monster called the Minotaur. A brave man called Theseus killed the monster.

The Minoan kings lived in a city called Knossos. Their palace was very luxurious, with beautifully decorated rooms. The queen had her own bathroom with running water. You can go and see this palace today. Some parts of the palace have been carefully rebuilt to show what it was like thousands of years ago.

The Minoans liked to watch the sport of bull-leaping. Teams of young men and women somersaulted over a bull's horns.

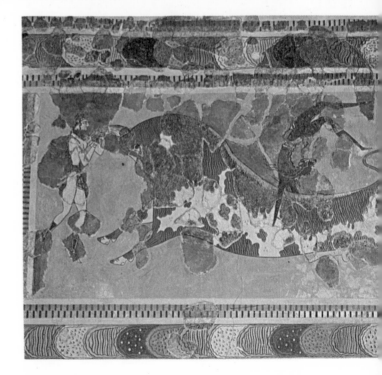

The Phoenicians were sea traders. Some sailed as far as West Africa to sell their cloth and metal goods.

The Phoenicians

The Phoenicians lived along the east coast of the Mediterranean, where they built ports like Tyre and Sidon. The Phoenicians were clever shipbuilders. They sailed across the Mediterranean and built cities like Carthage in North Africa.

The Phoenicians were skilled craftsmen. They carved figures in ivory, like this one, and made ornaments of coloured glass.

The Hittites

For a long time people used copper and bronze to make weapons and tools. The Hittites were among the first people to use iron. Iron is easier to make than bronze. It made cheaper tools and weapons.

The Hittites ruled a large empire for two hundred years. They defeated their enemies with iron weapons like those on the right.

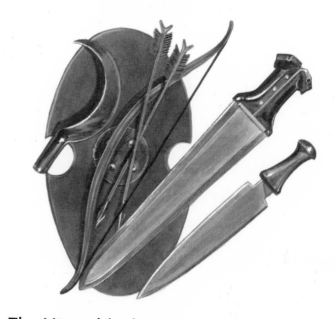

The Hittite blacksmiths were very important men. They made the iron weapons.

The Indus River cities

Even four thousand years ago some cities were like our cities today. Mohenjo-daro, a city by the River Indus, had drainage systems and plumbing. The houses had bathrooms. Water ran through clay pipes from a tank on the roof. In the picture you can see one of the city streets.

The Indus people bathed in public as well as at home. A public bath was a good place for friends to meet.

The Indus people worshipped many gods and goddesses. This statue is of a goddess.

This cart is carrying straw, which was used for making the roofs of houses in Mohenjo-daro. The cart has solid wooden wheels.

The Yellow River settlements

Just as in Ancient Egypt and in Mesopotamia, Chinese civilization first grew up by a great river. This was the Hwang-Ho, or Yellow River. Seven thousand years ago, the Chinese began to farm the land. Besides being farmers they were also skilled craftsmen.

The Chinese were very good at modelling in clay, bronze and jade. This dragon is made of bronze.

The Chinese grew rice and grain by the Hwang-Ho River. They cut canals leading from the river to bring water to their fields.

Chinese craftsmen used bronze to make weapons and ornaments. They made bronze from lead and tin. The two metals were heated until they melted and mixed together. Here, they are being poured into a mould.

The Assyrians

The Assyrians lived where the Sumerians had once lived, in Mesopotamia. The Assyrians were traders. They were often attacked as they carried their goods to other lands. So they had to fight many battles. Their soldiers became very important people.

The Assyrians invented many war machines. The battering ram was used for breaking down city walls.

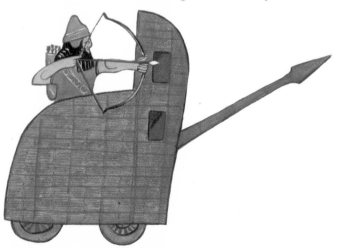

One of the greatest Assyrian kings was Assurbanipal. In the picture above he is hunting lions. Lions had to be killed because they destroyed cattle and sheep.

Assyrian archers fired iron tipped arrows at their enemies. In battle, groups of archers hid behind shields made of woven twigs. The shields could be moved around.

The Babylonians

The Ishtar Gate, which you can see here, was one of twelve gates that led into the city of Babylon. The gate is decorated with carvings of dragons and bulls. The Assyrians destroyed the city of Babylon, but it was later rebuilt. The city was rich and powerful under King Nebuchadnezzar.

Religion was very important to the Greeks. Zeus was their chief god.

Aphrodite, goddess of ~~love~~ crafts, was on of Zeus's daughters. *[annotation: "Athena" written above "Aphrodite", "crafts" written above "love"]*

The Greeks

The Greeks lived in south east Europe, over two thousand years ago. They built famous cities, like Athens and Sparta. Each city ruled itself. Sometimes one man ruled. Sometimes many men were in control.

The Greeks are famous for their artists and sculptors. This is a head of Aphrodite, a Greek goddess.

Apollo, the sun god, was a handsome son of Zeus.

Artemis, goddess of hunting, was another daughter of Zeus.

In Ancient Greece, a games contest was held every four years in Olympia. You can see a scene from one of these first Olympic games on the left.

The Greeks made beautiful vases. This one shows a scene from an old story about a hero called Odysseus.

The Seven Wonders of the World

About two thousand years ago a Greek writer made a list of the most remarkable buildings and statues in the world. They were called the Seven Wonders of the World. Today, all except one of the Seven Wonders have been destroyed or have crumbled into ruins. Only the pyramids of Egypt remain.

The picture on the right shows the Colossus of Rhodes. This was a huge statue of the Greek god Apollo. It stood by the harbour of Rhodes until an earthquake destroyed it.

Mausolus was a prince in Asia Minor. When he died his wife built him a huge tomb, shown below. It was called the Mausoleum.

Above are some of the pyramids of Egypt. The pyramids were royal tombs. They had rooms and passages inside them.

This enormous marble lighthouse, called the Pharos, was built by the Greeks in Egypt.

The Greeks built this temple to their goddess of hunting, Artemis. Seven hundred years before Christ, an attacking army burned the temple to the ground.

The picture below shows a statue of Zeus, king of the Greek gods. It was made of marble, gold and ivory. It stood at Olympia in Greece.

The Hanging Gardens of Babylon, in the picture above, were built by Nebuchadnezzar, king of Babylon. Water was pumped from ground level to the terraced gardens above.

THE ROMAN WORLD

The first Romans were farmers and warriors. They spread Roman rule through Italy about three hundred years before Christ. Later, the Emperor of Rome ruled half of Europe. He was the world's most powerful man.

Roman games were held in arenas like this one. Huge crowds of people came to watch the gladiators fighting.

The Roman army was the best trained army in the world. It was divided into groups, or legions. There were about six thousand men in each legion. Most soldiers fought on foot with short swords and javelins. A few soldiers rode horses.

Roman soldiers were not only good at fighting. They also built forts and roads in the lands they conquered. You can still see the remains of many of their buildings.

In a Roman city

One Roman city, called Pompeii, was
buried when a volcano erupted.
Many of the houses were preserved
under the ash, so we can find out a
lot about Roman buildings. In the city
there were grand houses, palaces,
temples and theatres. You can still
see the baths people washed in, and
wheel tracks in the road.

People lived very comfortably in Pompeii. They had fine furniture and heating underneath the floors.

When Pompeii was excavated, the shapes of the Romans who died there were found inside the hard ash.

Some buildings in Pompeii were only partly damaged when Vesuvius erupted. These wall paintings are almost as good as new.

Many of the streets of Pompeii were completely ruined, like the ones in the picture on the left. It must have been terrifying when the hot ash came raining down from the sky.

Some Celts built their villages on hill tops. In this picture they are fighting the Romans on the wooden pallisades, or fence.

The Celts

The Celts lived in tribes in central Europe, Britain and Ireland. When the Romans invaded Britain the Celts fought them fiercely.

The Romans defeated the Welsh and English Celts, but they could not conquer the Celts who lived in Scotland and Ireland.

Celtic chiefs and their wives often wore gold bands called torcs. They put the torcs around their necks.

Saxon nobles held feasts in great halls like this. They enjoyed listening to poets singing stories about Saxon heroes.

The Saxons

The Jutes, Angles and Saxons came from northern Europe. They invaded Britain after the Romans had left. They set up kingdoms in England and farmed in the lowlands where the crops grew well. The most famous Saxon king was Alfred the Great. He fought the Danes, who were attacking Britain.

One Saxon king was buried in his ship. This purse clasp was found among the treasures buried with him.

The Sack of Rome

For more than a thousand years, Rome was the most important city in Europe. Then in 410 an enemy army of Visigoths attacked. They broke down the city gates and destroyed the city. They set fire to the buildings, wrecked the monuments, stole treasures and killed many Romans. The Visigoths' attack is called the Sack of Rome.

R Phillips '78

The leader of the Visigoths was called Alaric. He said he would attack Rome if the Romans did not give him land and money. When they refused, he sacked the city.

NEW EMPIRES

Byzantium

The Roman Emperor Diocletian decided that his empire was too big to rule from one place. In 293 he divided the empire into two parts. One part was ruled from Rome, the other part from Byzantium. After Rome was sacked, the Byzantine empire became very important.

Byzantine churches were beautifully decorated with mosaic pictures. The mosaics were made out of squares of coloured stone pressed into the plaster on the walls.

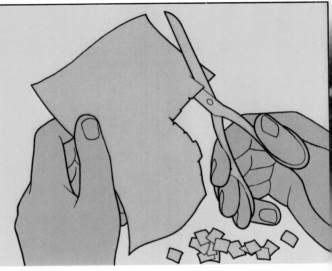

You could try making mosaic pictures. First, cut out tiny squares of paper of different colours. Or use pages from a magazine.

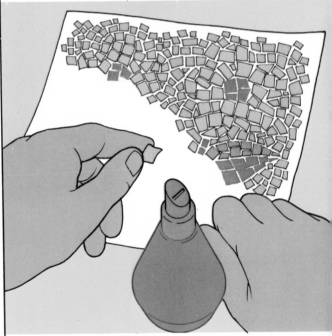

Then you can make a pattern or picture by sticking your coloured squares on to a piece of plain card. Use only tiny drops of glue.

The capital of the Byzantine Empire was called Constantinople after the Emperor Constantine. It had many fine buildings. In this picture you can see a procession and a market, too.

The rise of Islam

Muhammad was an Arabian who lived in Mecca. About six hundred years after the birth of Christ, he started a new religion, Islam. Today, it is the faith of most Arabs and many Africans and Asians. Mecca became the holy city of Muhammad's followers, the Muslims. The holy book Muslims use is called the Koran.

The Muslims built new cities like Baghdad in Iraq and Cairo in Egypt. They built domed temples, called mosques, for worshipping Allah.

Muslim armies conquered a great empire. In the big picture, Muhammad and his followers on the hill top are about to launch an attack.

The Vikings

The Vikings came by sea from Scandinavia to invade Britain and western Europe, in about the year 800. They burned down monasteries and houses and stole the treasures. Later they began to settle in the lands they had raided. Most Vikings lived on farms. They built long houses where their animals lived too.

The Vikings were great explorers. They discovered Greenland and some even reached North America.

The carved dragon's head on the left is from a Viking ship. The Vikings used figureheads like this to decorate their ships. They were skilful shipbuilders. They made wide-bodied ships for trading and long narrow ships for raiding.

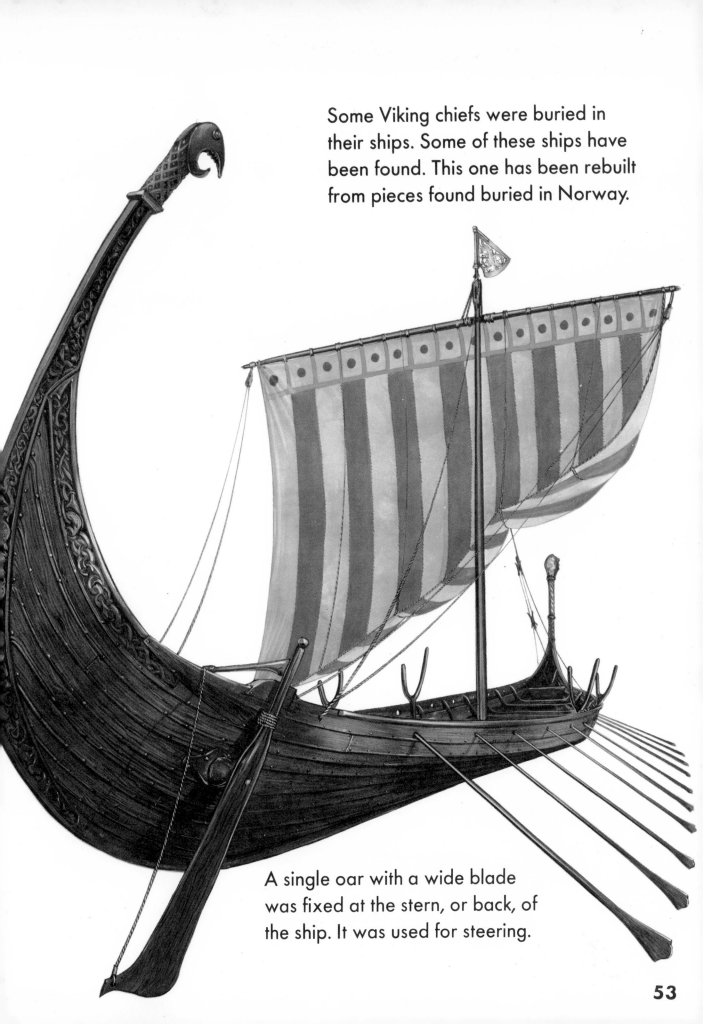

Some Viking chiefs were buried in their ships. Some of these ships have been found. This one has been rebuilt from pieces found buried in Norway.

A single oar with a wide blade was fixed at the stern, or back, of the ship. It was used for steering.

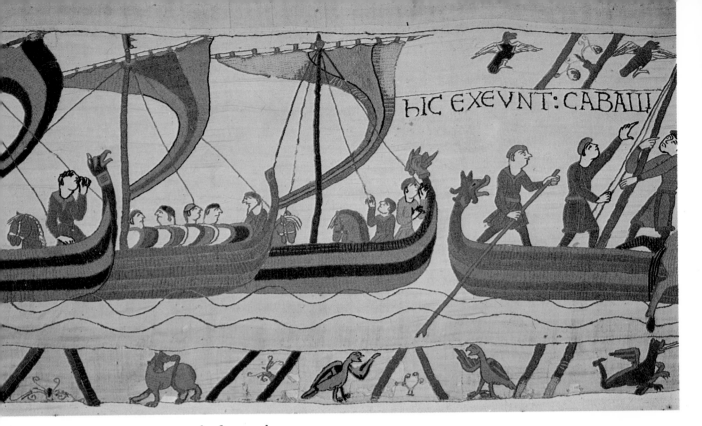

HIC EXEVNT:CABALL

Here are two panels from the Bayeux Tapestry. The embroidered pictures tell the story of the Norman Conquest of England in 1066.

The Normans

The Norman Duke William invaded England because he believed that England should belong to him. The English wanted their own king, Harold. William defeated Harold at the Battle of Hastings. Afterwards, William built great castles like this one to guard his new kingdom. This castle is made of stone.

turrets

chapel

well

main entrance

54

ON RA AN GLORVM EXER ACI TV

In the lefthand panel you can see some Norman ships. In the panel above some knights of William, Duke of Normandy, are fighting.

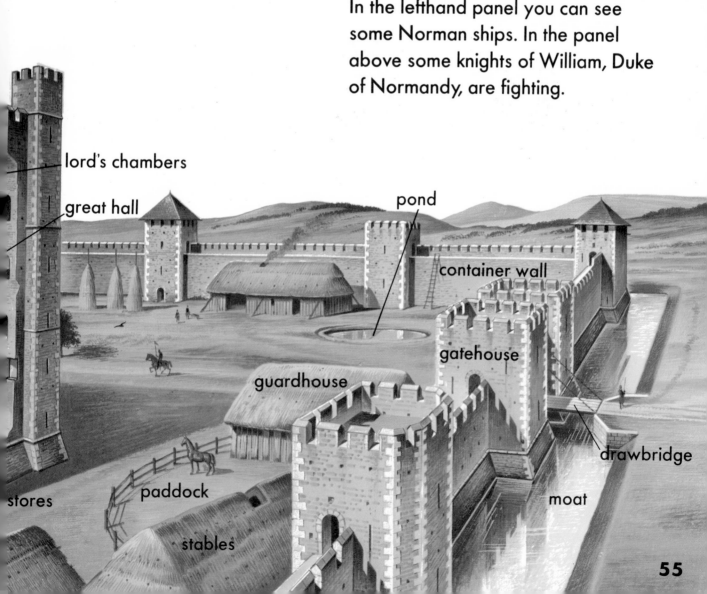

lord's chambers

great hall

pond

container wall

gatehouse

guardhouse

drawbridge

stores

paddock

moat

stables

55

The Great Wall of China is wide enough for troops to march along the top.

The Chinese

Chinese civilization stayed much the same for over four thousand years. In Ancient China, people thought of the Emperor as a god. They obeyed the Emperor and his officials without question. Anyone who disobeyed was harshly punished. Most Chinese farmers were poor and had to work long and hard for a living.

Chinese craftsmen liked carving figures out of jade, like this horse.

The Chinese used black gunpowder to make fireworks. They held exciting firework displays in their cities.

The Chinese invented the compass four thousand years ago. It was not used anywhere else for hundreds of years.

The Chinese probably invented printing. The printer cut out letters in a block of wood. He inked the block and pressed a sheet of paper on it.

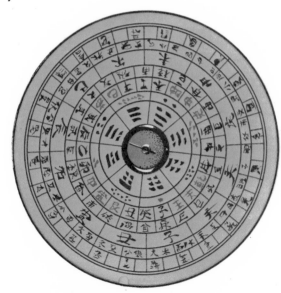

The Mongols

The Mongols were cattle farmers in Central Asia. They moved from place to place to find good farmland.

This is Genghis Khan, who became leader of the Mongols. Khan means 'chief ruler.' Genghis was one of the greatest rulers in history.

The Great Wall of China was built to keep out invaders. But the armies of Genghis Khan broke through it. They conquered most of northern China.

Genghis Khan formed armies of horsemen. They charged into enemy towns, set fire to them and rode off before anyone could stop them.

Genghis Khan's armies invaded Russia too. His empire became so big that it took him a year to cross it from end to end.

Kublai Khan was the grandson of Genghis. Kublai became ruler of Genghis's huge empire in 1260. In this picture he is receiving visitors.

The Japanese

Long ago, people came to Japan from nearby islands, and from China. They were fishermen and hunters. Then invaders came to Japan. One of the invaders became the first emperor of Japan. He was called Jimmu.

For over six hundred years, Samurai warriors ruled Japan. They were very brave soldiers and people were afraid of them. Their armour was made of hundreds of iron links.

The Japanese made houses of bamboo and beautiful gardens with rocks, sand and trees. In this picture, an emperor is sitting in his garden.

On the left you can see Japanese ladies carrying out the Tea Ceremony. This is a way of welcoming guests.

The Maya

The Maya lived in Central America, a thousand years ago. Their farmers grew maize. The Maya were clever astronomers and mathematicians.

The Maya built pyramids, like the Egyptians. The pyramids were temples for their gods.

DID YOU KNOW?

The Vikings were very clean people. They wore special nightgowns and slept in beds in the walls of their houses.

A rich Muslim ruler who loved toys once had a tree with leaves made of pure gold. Toy birds stood on the branches, singing like real ones.

A Roman writer said that a spider's web soaked in vinegar and oil would stop a wound bleeding. It may sound messy, but it really works!

INDEX